The
Agenda

RED ELK

ISBN-13: 978-1482071016
ISBN-10: 1482071010

DEDICATION

To the reader.

Table of Contents

INTRODUCTION

This book is correspondence Red Elk had with another person after the "terrorist attack" on 911.

Friend(s):

To help you not feel "slapped" by the information you are about to read, I would like to lead you into it in a more "eased" way. The pages ahead can shock (the "slap" told of).

I began my medicine learning at age ten. It was foretold this would be at age four. My learning lasted 41 years before I was allowed to work in this field. Some lessons lasted for years before completed. Included in this grouping was how to be so CLOSE TO THE CREATOR I could know His mind. It is this teaching that has allowed "The Agendas" to be. Diligent searching through prayer, asking, and seeking has brought about the information contained in the next pages. These things did not come easily, but they DID come!

These pages will do nothing but make you AWARE or at least think. Are they possible? For you only time will tell. For me THERE IS <u>NO TIME</u> AND ARE TRUE.

"Not only has our world become smaller, but so too all without. Galaxies and universes are now as readily traveled by others as we do with our aircraft around our own world."

"Destination? EARTH!"

Ho,

Red Elk

THE AGENDA

It is 5:00 a.m. and I am in town with my "coffee" (diet Pepsi). I am finally getting caught up from my Canadian trip. It sure wore me out. From 8:30 a.m. to 2:30 a.m. I was teaching for five days in a row. It just wiped me out. To get there and back took 23 hours, but what a view into the Kootenay Mountain Range, it was beautiful. They are like a cross between our Rockies and Sweden's Alps. I had no idea they existed.

Canada seems so DEPRESSED though. It was like going into a police state or World War II Germany. Taxes are out of sight. Wages are very low. People are cutting corners to survive, cheating each other just to keep even and to live. And we are headed in the

EXACT SAME DIRECTION! I can't believe the Canadians haven't rebelled and overthrown their controlling government, but then I am surprised we haven't done the same here, too. What Canada is, the world will be, and other countries I hear are even worse. You can EXPECT that out of a dictator ran country, but a CIVILIZED one? What a shock! Yes, I dread where we are going.

Ho.

It seems Canada follows England, i.e., "the Queen." Well, that crown wears scales and is either a half breed or controlled willingly by none other than our "friendly" outside and inside "gods," i.e., reptilian race. Damn our governments that have allowed this deception to take forth in the first place. Until now we of earth have been over ran by these idiots. AB bloodlines, small chested, large belly and belly breathers.   It is not hard to spot them; men of the half

breed especially. They are a domineering bunch. They

like to live by mind, not physical. They supervise, and

are not blue collar workers. They just don't like

physical work! It is

"beneath" them. The gals glom onto "uprising" human

males and to those who are going "into" something,

i.e., (males going into money making opportunities).

"Lawyers" seem to be a favorite "for me" match. Then

the gals use others of their breeding to catapult their

human mate into a place of power (control);

politicians, higher police positions, military, etc. All

those are controlling positions over our earth's masses.

It is a very deliberate, cunning take over.

Time means little to them. The goal is what

matters. And that goal started ages ago when they

colonized a planet's "interior" lands; their inner lands.

Here – ten to say thousands of years ago, at least past our earth's last three flips.

Again, the goal (to rule) is the agenda and it always has been.

Why? To control our planet's minerals, water sources, human food, DNA, farming, and slavery. It is just simply to DOMINEER. Not only us (and other planets) but to be the galaxies' (several) <u>commercial leaders,</u> and be the galaxies' <u>GODS</u> (the BIG "G").

They are very egotistical people and very single minded. I call this the "WE ARE GOD" complex.

Pretty heady. Yet all their eons of planets' infiltration will not succeed in the end and that end is VERY NEAR. Oh, there will be a comeback try but even that won't work! THE TRUE AND ONLY GOD just won't allow it.

10

Ho.

These Reptilians are in alliance with three other planetary groups. The Bee people ("Grays" to most), a Gargoyle race, and a strange (other dimensions) group (race) of beings which are large, hairy, super intelligent "SASQUATCH" type giants that I find difficult to see due to their aura of the dimension they cross to get here to work with the "unholy (domineering) alliance." Rarely is this aura crossover unsuccessful, i.e., rare to see them in "all physical" form. They carry this aura with them, i.e., not a full crossover. For some reason they seem to hinder "full" crossover, as it is a danger to them, and then they use this dimension aura as a weapon of personal safety. This is effective, too! If they are shot while in this crossover form, they disappear, or "bounce," or waiver. It is magical. It is damn hard to kill them, but it is not as easy for them

11

when they are in "full" form though. That is when they are vulnerable. I think our "U.S." black-ops units (all humans) have machined a way to strip some of these into "full here" form, i.e., no "dimension" ability. Trapped. Ho.

Anyway, these lanky "hairy ones" come from a dimension our scientists know nothing about. They are aware that dimensions exist, looking like a bending slightly twisting "ribbon" in the creation of creation. They see this ribbon as two sided: the front and the back. But they are failing to see it has five sides, the front/back and two <u>edges</u> and more, i.e., the "Ribbon" is a flattened out SQUARE WITH AN <u>INSIDE</u>!

So they look only at two sides. There is a WHOLE LOT OF "OTHERS" OUT THERE WHO LIVE ON THE EDGE(S) AND IN! There is a fascinating group of "hidden" beings and one kept secret (sacred knowledge) by the most elite of the "holy" men/women of all the Federation of Planets…the "1,000,000."

Yes, even the Federation has its "masons" and "moose" type hierarchy of societies just as your white people do, and we Native Americans do and native Africans do, etc., etc.

I find these ribbon "edge(s) and center" difficult to see, but it is seeable once you are aware of their existence. Ho.

You have got to be a "Columbus" to know/find these things, i.e., go beyond what is the "norm" of mass thought.

We have too many blind sheep leading the blind sheep.

Ho.

When one begins to SEE, they are slapped

down or ostracized from the group. Too bad, ALL the sheep could SEE if they would just open their eyes!

Ho.

Okay, now we have two of the four unholy alliance groups understood. Now for the "Grays" and Gargoyles. Oops, but back first to the "Ribbon Edger's"–why are they into this? Again: domination and to commercialize. They (the "sasquatch") who are of the edges of the unseen dimension in time (same as the <u>other</u> three) are trying to gain control OVER the other three. ALL FOUR HAVE THIS IN MIND, i.e., back biting! Each of the four wants to be the "God." So not only are they in alliance to control <u>ALL</u> but each is maneuvering to make sure THEIR race controls all, <u>including the other three.</u>

Okay the "Grays"– there are not many of them left. Most of which is seen are parasite DRONES!

MADE beings. They are made by the REAL ONES. The real ones are taller and lankier and are the "brains" of these made colonies of beings. These clones are the real one's "hope" to carry on their race and to use as personal soldiers. Basically these parasites are a form of robots. Intelligent robots of plant fiber base. They are grown just as we grow a garden and harvested to do the work needed.

Oh, it is much more complicated than said, but the idea is the same. A grown parasite robot with LIFE and INTELLIGENCE and controlled by their makers. The makers are the ones that "count" for their true bloodline race is dying. This was caused long ago over their desire to overcome the emotion of hate and anger. In so doing, all emotions were eliminated, including love and that included sexual desire love (no emotions and no erections).

They had to revert to "dish" (test tube) babies. In time, their females began dying off for LACK OF EMOTIONAL LOVE--including their own and their mates. One literally dies, dying because of "emptiness." Emotions are mandatory to and for GOD LIFE. Without it, it ceases erection/ejection and egg dropping. What once was "good" became/becomes just NOTHING in the sperm and eggs and in time just quits existing. So the sex act stops. Emotional lack also kills the "spirit" of life and it dries up. If there is no emotion, there is no continuance of race.

The Reptilian race doesn't have this problem. Ruled by women of the species, the males are sex "workhorses." They are sent to interact with the females of the planets for subvert colonizing. The half breeds are then "minded" into the Lizz agenda. Not all of them accept this and become more human than the humans of that planet they are bred upon. I know two of these.

The Lizz, breeding between them, have large eggs. I don't know their incubation period, but know they are well tended, usually by volunteers and slaves.

The Grays? So far I have yet to meet a female. I don't know if they exist any longer. I have seen males though of the true race. What I have seen appear to be scientists or doctors. They are always busy trying to experiment with our earth man's DNA and their own parasite (smaller) creation. There seems to be an urgency about this for their race ("trues") is near extinction. As for that, eons ago this race split. There are now three planets of them: one totally "bad," and the others at least BETTER. A world civil war was averted due to this split. The

"goods" agreeing to colonize somewhere else. These

"goods" are now in the process of colonizing yet another planet. They keep an eye on what their "dark" (original planet) brothers are doing and are ready to take advantage of their "dark" DNA by successful efforts even if it means death and war between the two. As usual, domination is the "rule."

Our planets are full of back biters. This extends into multitudes of planes, times, and dimensions, Creation wide.

Now for the Gargoyles: They are probably the WORST beings in all creation. These are true renegades: horrible beings in looks and in "spirit." They are so bad it is hard to call them humans. But as all the Creator's children they too, have souls. All humans, regardless of what they look like (caused by the environment they live in) have souls.

These Gargoyle beings are the "Al Capones" of

18

the four in the "unholy four" alliance. "We get our cut or we cut you!" was and is their "motto." The other three use them to their advantage and vice-versa. Naturally plans are always underway by the other three to get these (fourth) out of the way. Again, war looms always. Inner sabotage is constantly going on.

The Gargoyles live on a "space ship," which is their <u>PLANET</u>! This planet roams, touching the area on planets they "farm." And farm they do, in raids…raiding for that planet's humans. Our lovely Gargoyles are meat eaters and WE are the meat they eat…preferably alive! They specialize in eating children alive, in front of the child's parents.

GARGYLES DOTE ON FEAR! To them it is like a good steak sauce on their meat. Fear-giving is their motivation and prime <u>emotion</u>. They thrive on it and it gives them exceedingly long life.

This emotion literally "excites" them into a sexual frenzy between them and their captive(s). Rape and fear make them into madmen/madwomen creating even more madness, until the Gargoyles' are exhausted or their rape victims (male or female) are dead.

As their planet roams (a big oval path) they send out raiders as "walk-ins." These are advance guards, "the point men." These raiders prepare the planet they are approaching by taking over instantly dead and/or willing <u>LIVE</u> people, of the approached planet. They are so magnetic in personality while using these walked-in bodies (possession) that it is easy to gain a following amongst those they are about to raid. These followers in turn become possessed, actually ENTERED, by ONE RAIDER, i.e., one raider splits into <u>numerous</u> live bodies until a mass of "humans" are there to convince their worlds' people these "coming aliens are good and friends despite their looks." A setup and always believed.

Their ships are rather short ranged, i.e., their planet is very close when they arrive as "the good guys despite their looks." Then the trap is sprung and the "reaping of the harvest" begins.

They always leave survivors. They are the "seeds" for the next century's growth for their next arrival/harvest. This is where our stories/tales of such beings derive from: fact not fiction, truth not fairy tales or folklore, and their vanguards are <u>HERE RIGHT NOW</u>!

Yes, a real mean bunch. As close to demons as humans can get without being one!
Ho.

MANY OF THE LIZARDS ARE THE SAME WAY. These Reptilians are not too far behind in evolution from the Gargoyles. Many are "pushing it" as they like the POWER feeling these deeds do.   It is much like our "skinheads" of today. Deeds that are done for the POWER OF IT!

Ho.

So there you are – four unholy alliance groups and their agenda for us. And why? "God Ship" through commerce.

The Lizzy's use the Grays as their "dirty" boys. Lizards don't like getting their "hands dirty." Believing themselves superior, they use the Grays. The Grays, feeling superior, allow themselves to be used thinking they can "con" the Lizards. After all, they can always grow more parasites. Meanwhile the true Grays ("bee/insect" people) are going like mad raping our DNA via abductions for their experiment to get back emotions. And they in turn are being watched and possibly warred upon by their long left "good" brothers who think they are superior to their "bad" ones. So they let the "bad" do the dirty work and pounce when the time is right.

The Gargoyles basically "don't give a damn." They say, "We are in this or you are out." They are hardball players more than capable of cutting the other three's throats to become the "Gods" and planning to do this.

Those of the "Ribbon Edge" are in this to take over HERE and use THIS knowledge on/in their OWN dimension and DO the same thing there and thus be even BIGGER "GODS."

"ALL CONTROLLING GODS."

Things are coming to a head here for us (earth). The Reptilians are now so confident they have control over enough of our leaders they have ordered open mining of our resources to begin and it is being so done now–very brazen.

Meanwhile, the bee (Grays) parasites themselves are getting a grip on being "human" and a new race is starting to be. It is one that is about to rebel against their makers (the "trues") and THEMSELVES become "GOD."

"Yup, win against the masters, and then we'll take on the rest."

War, war, war.

Then there are those who could care less. Too bad, like it or not, these events will not be ignored. <u>All</u> will become involved. War is coming creation wide.

So you know "the agenda" and the why of all the UFO's, abductions, strange activities, and blackouts. You know.

Oh no, no you don't, not yet! For this is just

24

the <u>seen</u> agenda.

THERE IS A STEALTH MOVEMENT ON WHAT THE ALIEN AGENDA IS – AND WHAT <u>REALLY</u> IS!

For you see, there is another wanting to be "God," and it is THIS ONE who is BEHIND THE <u>SEEN</u> AGENDA. This one and his followers are masters of Stealth–High Masters! You are not going to like what you are about to read. Many will toss this down in disdain and in disgust because you simply <u>refuse</u> to believe what all this is about, but you wanted to know. PhD's have wanted to know. Men of God have wanted to know. The greatest and the least have wanted to know. This being, the one many speak of and still ignore, this very real and living being is LUCIFER!

His followers are those that left God's land

eons and eons ago after a failed attempt at overthrowing the ONE and ONLY GOD.

The Gargoyles were his first successful humankind takeover. The Lizards were number two. In time, his generals have succeeded in infiltrating ALL times, dimensions, and planes. <u>ALL!</u> NOT ONE EXISTS WITHOUT INFILTRATION. NONE!

The "seen" agenda is this "master's" DESIGNED agenda…Or so he thinks! NOT SO! The true designer is our <u>CREATOR HIMSELF</u>. For you see, Armageddon is due soon. But it is NOT ON EARTH ALONE, but in the HEAVENS (again) as well, i.e., a DOUBLE ARMAGEDDON. The battle of the eons and: "There was war in the Heavens".

Folks, it never really stopped but now it returns to one spot--us! And it comes to us full bore! EVERYONE in creation will be involved. Even to those who have done their best not to get involved.

A few months ago I was contacted by members of the Federation of Planets. They informed me our planet was to be invaded and taken over by these planets for we were the cause of (they believe) a split within the Federation that will cause war between all within the Federation and thus "heaven wide." WE MUST BE CONTROLLED OR KILLED.

THIS IS THE AGENDA: WAR BETWEEN THE REAL GOD AND THE ONE WHO STILL WANTS TO BE.

It is Lucifer's BIG PUSH. His calling in of all his followers against our Creator's followers. MASS DEATH sky wide and heaven deep. Millions coming together to battle it out and about zero who are aware it is this that they are here for! A mass gathering of: good versus evil.

"HE COMES AS A ROARING LION."

You see friends; it is not just a "big push." It is also Lucifer's last "hurrah." FOR HE ALREADY KNOWS HE HAS LOST! It is a war of destruction! Lucifer will destroy as many

of God's people as possible so that only a smoldering mess remains as fried and polluted planets, bones in space and on planets, etc., – UTTER DESTRUCTION!

For if he, "can't have it, no one will!" And if someone does have it, it isn't worth having.

THERE IS YOUR AGENDA AND THERE IS THE WHY OF IT – HATE.

Earth is a "mousetrap" in space and WE are the bait! For we are the only ones left with the GOD knowledge of all the roots. The agenda is angels and man fighting side by side, some

for good and some for evil: the Two Armageddon's.

28

<u>Now</u> you know, "THE AGENDA."

Ho.

   At least in the two agendas, there is still the

Ultimate (GOD) Agenda. That too is known and will

be shared at a later date.

Ho,

Red Elk

THE ULTIMATE GOAL - THE GOD AGENDA

This is the "why" of all that is going as it is. It is not easy to understand to those who have no God belief or are hindered by rhetoric of teaching or any other numerous reasons. Still, it is the way of it…the WHY.

Yes, it sounds heady on my part. I don't make the rules though; I just report them. So much is involved with this…years of learning to connect with the Creator far and above the average Christian doing. Though Christians are taught in the scriptures, near none see it, let alone use it. We of medicine do though. It was taught 2000 years ago, then passed down to us today. I do teach this way, but that is not what this writing is about. This is about the FINDING, or rather, FIND. It is quite possible for anyone to find this as well if you just hunger/knock/seek. THEN YOU WILL FIND!

It all started at the beginning when only the Creator was…nothing else. I suppose "He" (no sex) was bored or just wanted to do something other than just BE. I don't know, but it started . . . the creating.

He (I'm using "He" as this seems to be the most accepted reference to our Creator) first made angels: beings to counteract his boredom, then planets and humans to populate them, including all that that life supports its needs. Our earth but one of many, this creation goes into multitudes of dimensions and planes and eventually even into parallel times.

In time there was rebellion amongst the heavens and angels ("war in the heavens"). The Great "chess game" had begun: two major opponents against each other – one vying to be God and one who WAS.

One-third of the aggressors left with him. This one named Lucifer. All others sided and stayed with the Creator. Ho.

The Creator wanted <u>all</u> to see what kind of "God" this wannabe would be if "GOD." And thus sin (disobedience to God) entered into all the worlds.

Lucifer came to one planet; this one we call ours: Earth. He still resides here deep within us. There are six "worlds" in all. Five within ours and number one is all molten lava. He cannot live there, but loves heat. His headquarters and dwelling places are on/in the next "ball" – number two. (We are number six). It is here all his orders go out to all his angel generals. Each a "sub-ruler" of a (+) planet, in all dimensions, etc.

For your information, the perfect planet heat

wise, etc., WAS the one between us and our sun (other than Mercury and Venus). Hoping to throw his pursuers (God's angels) off, he destroyed this planet, came to ours, and bored into its depths until his comfort zone was met. In time all lived-on planets were "seeped" into by Lucifer's forces. Sin entered into all creation.

And in time some of these planetary brothers went fully to the "dark," i.e., satanic-like. Others became "good," others a bit of each, and others just didn't evolve one way or another. Overtime whole planets have died and are extinct, but the Creator keeps creating. It is a never ending circle.
Ho.

Only ONE planet kept its God roots. US/Ours! And all know how hard it is here to be "good." It is easier (and most believe more fun) to sin. Slowly

Lucifer is strangling us off. Armageddon will slow that. The <u>next</u> cleansing will halt it forever. (This is still over 1,000 years away). But why is our Creator letting this all GO On? It is easy being He is a "just and loving God," if He simply took Lucifer and his followers out of His thoughts (total death forever) he would be a dictator and NOT a "just and loving" God. HE IS WAITING FOR ANGELS TO COME TO HIM (as a group of speakers for all His angels) with a request to put a stop to it!

In short, THEY MUST BE CONVINCED <u>TOTALLY</u> that Lucifer would NOT BE BETTER THAN GOD! HE IS WAITING FOR THEM TO PETITION HIM!

If He, on His own, did away with Lucifer and his angel followers, well, all the two-third remaining angels would FEAR HIM, i.e., "What if I COUGHED in His presence? What if I did something wrong? WILL HE JUST DO AWAY WITH ME TOO?"

Fear, not LOVE, would "rule" in their hearts and constant "walking on eggs."

This is NOT a LOVE GOD. And GOD <u>IS</u> <u>LOVE</u>. Total pure LOVE!

Ho.

Some may ask why then not do away with Lucifer's "badness," i.e., forgive him.

Number one, even angels have will, i.e., to do as THEY will; and number two, Lucifer DOESN'T <u>WANT</u> forgiveness, he WANTS TO BE THE GOD THAT RULES <u>ALL</u>. Don't believe it? Look around.

And the God angels will get tired of it. They will just get fed up and ask God, "Please put a stop to it." It is THEN it will be so.

Ho.

There friends is the "WHY."

Now, I can just hear, "IT ISN'T FAIR! WHY should we suffer," and on and on and on. You see you are so GROUNDED in your skin that that is the only "skin" you think about, "Protect my hide" attitude. This would be fine and good if our "earth body" was immortal. It isn't, but our SOUL IS. LIFE GOES ON!

Immortality exists in our <u>soul</u>, not our <u>body</u>. So why fight so hard to "live" when immortal life is <u>beyond</u> this one? I do not understand you. Especially you Christians who claim to believe in life after death. When death looks into your eyes, you panic. WHY DO YOU FEAR? You must not believe as much as you think, huh?

This does not mean you are to seek death. NO! But just look beyond body death and become "as one" NOW in your heart with our Creator. You can

EXPERIENCE HEAVEN here on EARTH <u>NOW</u> and CONTINUE THIS INTO THE NEXT PLANE UP (heaven) upon your departure here.

DEATH IS A CONTINUATION OF LIFE (only in a more POWERFUL form). WHAT YOU LEARN THERE YOU <u>CAN</u> LEARN <u>HERE</u>. Ho.

So why do you allow yourself to LIVE IN YOUR OWN HELL!

"I have come that you may have life and that ABUNDANTLY." - (Jesus/N.T.)

Ho.

Red Elk

NEW YORK BOMBINGS

I would like to share with you about the terrorist attacks on America. What I am about to say is so unbelievable, so "fantastic", so lunatic; you will honestly believe I have lost my mind (literally).

So far in my years of writing to you I have told nothing but truths. I am continuing to do so even though what I am about to write is far out.

I believe I shared with you that many months ago I was visited by a small factor of the "Council of 1,000,000"– who came to inform me that the Federation of Planets have voted to invade earth and that it would take two or three years to formulate before being carried out. They sought my advice. This in New York was PART OF THAT PREPARATION! What you and 99-1/2% of earth's people are unaware

38

of is at this very moment a GIGANTIC WAR is taking place in space. One involves THOUSANDS of ships. It has taken us ("the group"– and those from the rebels of other planets who are helping us/all) by surprise. It will be about two or three more weeks before the outcome of this war will be known. In the ultimate roots of this battle, it will be found out if this war is/has occurred.

This space war is instigated by the Dracolians, backed by the other three of the "unholy" four and ultimately by Lucifer himself. ALL, the "four" AND those fighting them are fighting OVER OUR "BONES!" A very few on the side against the four are in this not for our bones, but to hold some form of peace within the extensive galaxies. Not "for" us, but to keep peace, however fragile.

You see, the Dracolians (Lizard race) are

making a move on us and it's not too well

received by the others who lay claim to us via DNA,

too. The Dracolians are trying to grab "all the PIE" (us

of this planet).

There are two factors of Dracolians–both

governed by females: the Queens. These two and

theirs' have been at war against us all millenniums.

These same two factors are the "human" factors that

are calling claim to us…our "masters." ALL our

earth's governments have been deeply infiltrated by

both sides of this factor. WE DO NOT control us, they

do. And they are quite brazen about it, exposing

themselves nearly openly now in their confidence we

are a defeated world.

Soon (months, weeks, years?)…One of these

Queen's ships will appear over our skies. "Enormous,"

in size does not do it justice in description. The

"conquering hero" will return (from this space war) to "close the fight" with a final battle against her rival here on earth, Armageddon. All planets will be involved. That involvement is NOW, in this great space war. It is not only <u>just</u> coming to us, but IS HERE NOW! The New York bombing is THE TWO QUEEN FACTORS GOING AGAINST EACH OTHER NOW <u>HERE</u>! They are maneuvering for final overthrow of each other in the last battle. Unfortunately, that last battle is on THIS planet and naturally involves every human here.

We of earth are so INGRAINED on BOTH SIDES (of the Lizzards) we humans of earth are <u>easily</u> controlled to do either side's bidding–the terrorists' blind sheep, soldiers WHO ARE LED BY LIZZARDS IN DISGUISE! The Lizzards (of both sides) are HIGH MASTERS of CONTROLLING EMOTIONS OF

MAN (earth/others). It is in this sabotage they conquer.

Lizzards are extremely long lived. Their high commands have/hold secrets of longevity even far beyond their normal races' people (who amongst themselves live hundreds of years).

Both the opposing Queens are tens of <u>THOUSANDS</u> of years old. These "high ones" are much like our Dali Lama, who "stays tuned" to a new energy (new baby body) that is about to be born bringing BOTH the TONEL and NAGUAL "bodies" into the new energy body about to be born. Thus the Dali Lama remains the same person in each "jump" keeping all the old remembrances and adding the new body's lifetime(s) knowledge.

These two Queens do likewise; "jumping." Neither they or the Dali Lama know this way of "remembered pasts" are not necessary to do (as they do), it is simply, simple and easy to do on another scale, that of duality of spirit.

Anyway, the two Queens are about to meet and fight (the final fight) right here on and above/over our planet. The emotions of our planet's people are (and have been) being manipulated at this (New York) time. IT IS THE TWO Queens' earth humans CONTROLLED FACTORS that has brought the NEW YORK TERRORIST ATTACKS ABOUT! <u>US</u> controlled by two warring Queens: to dominate earth (and eventually all creation). The winner "takes ALL."

What this world sees as man against man in these world events is actually man against man CONTROLLED BY LIZZARD AGAINST LIZZARD!

Our next earth event will be the God showing of our (earth/us) UNTURNABLE PATH: the sign of a

BLOOD RED SKY. It will be VERY SOON AFTER that the next major event will occur: the FALSE RAPTURE. Just a few months or years (two to three) after that, the TRUE RAPTURE will occur. THAT one to save God's true heart people, from the Great Death Battle, between the forces of Christ and the forces of Lucifer in spirit and in physical (i.e., physical people and spirit beings).

WHAT IS OCCURRING NOW – (today/New York) – is THE GATHERING OF ALL CREATION'S PHYSICAL BEINGS to THIS AREA OF THE ALL GALAXIES and eventually to one corner of the ONE galaxy, i.e., US. Armageddon. And the true battle, GOD VERSUS LUCIFER.

The ultimate show down will take place probably "within" the next eleven years. POSSIBLY YET even further away (depending on OUR ability to

"get right" with GOD). However, it <u>will</u> BE! I "see"
Armageddon from approximately 2012 to as late as
2026 (or rather 2025-2026).

So, ahead is: THE RED SKY

                       FALSE RAPTURE

                       WAR (World War III?)

(Not sure which   LUCIFER IN MAN

   FORM

will be first here)   THE ROLLING OF

                       EARTH (#5 Roll)

                       TRUE RAPTURE

                       ARMAGEDDON

All being lined up now thanks to our "friendly"
Dracolian/other three race(s) and by the multitudes of
other world beings. ULTIMATELY by GOD
HIMSELF who is tired of this bickering, "nibbling"
and unfaithfulness of his chosen children

(Jews/Christians). It is about to come to an end.

As for His "unfaithful" it is NOT a case of being unfaithful, but a case of being UNFOLLOWING due to a lack of faith/trust and BLIND FOLLOWING of false leaders (in synagogues and churches) caused by LAZINESS.

Lucifer has spent years cultivating our minds to this end: REDUCING OUR SPIRITUAL AWARENESS OF RIGHTFUL FIGHTING AND ABILITY TO DO GOD'S ABILITY (AGAPE) LOVE THINGS/WORKS! We (Christians/Jews) are NOW "right" (in mind and weak spirit) FOR THIS FINAL BATTLE!

We are very weak.

Thus he (Lucifer) is STRONG!

Now, the final battle is soon upon us. He (Lucifer) thinks he is strong enough to win. If not, he intends to take as many "down" as he can in his defeat. Striking as a stricken/wounded LION. He knows there is no death until the final death but will RIP AND SHRED (hurt physically) as many as he can on his way "down" the (defeated) trail.

There's more; there is a very ancient Native prophecy concerning this "end" time. Somehow I have evidently become a key player in it. It concerns my work with the many ancient pyramids I have become, "The Keeper Of."

"In those days, 'The Keeper' will find the key pyramid and bring it into play (use). When this is done all our earth's vibration will change. Many (people) will go mad (crazy) as they are not of the right heart to change (to this vibration change). Many will die. The world will become madness. This will bring in the "ending" (of civilization as we know it). It will be the time of madness, change, LOVE, and repair (of the people). A piece of the star brothers' way of travel (spaceship) will be used. The Teacher (Christ) will return to finish this work."

I own that piece. Ho.

It came three days ago with orders to return to the key pyramid I have found and totally change (heal) its aiming device.

Later: I was there two weeks with one day repairing, but had a problem with the aiming device. With the orders came too the instructions on completing the work to total perfection. I must now return and do that work (since have done so).

So, all "Hell" is about to break loose. It will/is anyway and my role in this is to make sure of its AFTER outcome. Those who survive this aftermath will in time dominate earth with "pure heart", i.e., GOD SPIRITUALITY. A BIG

CHANGE is ahead BEYOND Armageddon.

Ho.

Red Elk

NEW YORK: GOD'S WILL?

Many has asked me, 'WHY!?" Or said, "What kind of God is THIS who would allow such a thing!?"

Others have said, "It must be\is God's will."

All three sayings are answerable.

"Why?"

Because this Great Creator will not take away our gift: personal will.

"Why?"

Because we of the earth masses have willed to do as WE PLEASE TO SERVE SELF! We choose OUR way of SELF over HIS of PURE LOVE.

Not all have so chosen, but we are too few to make right over wrong. The majority rules.

"Why would a GOD allow this?"

Because number 1: the above; and number 2:

TO WARN!

Just as "holding" hate/fear/etc. allows sickness to enter our bodies (self-brought illnesses), so too, as Metalkwa Ooshin (<u>ONE</u>) the same brings wars and mass destruction on we ONE as a whole. A warning to ALL OF EARTH we are NOT Right – (right standing -- "righteousness") in the Creator's sight, i.e., "HOLDING"–as ONE. Get right--all body illnesses disappear. Get right–all worlds "ONE" wars, etc. disappear.

It is as simple as that.

<u>WE</u> made this to be.

He won't take away our will.

BUT:

He warns–because He <u>CARES</u> FOR US!

New York is a <u>WARNING</u>!

It will get worse IF WE DON'T RETURN TO

LOVE.

It's HIS way of spanking us to awareness of our wrong path we are taking!

A harsh lesson?

To the majority, yes.

But remember: THERE IS NO DEATH.

Those of the New York/D.C./Pennsylvania horrors are ALIVE and IN HIS ARMS, His homeland. It's just THEIR sacrifice to us, (subconsciously done by each) so WE, "LEFT BEHIND," can FEEL/KNOW the SPANKING and the why of it.

Will we listen?

So far, NO. We war, not LOVE.

Send out the SINGERS and we ALL win. Go on the way we are, as a pouting, revengeful child, and the next "spanking" WILL BE HARDER!

Not because our Creator is not there, or mean,

or we are his puppets, etc., but because HE CARES.

HE LOVES US!

Are we, have we, over the centuries been

GOOD children?

YOU answer that.

Now as for: "God's will."

Bull!

GOD'S WILL IS COMPASSION,

FORGIVENESS, LOVE!

THAT'S God's will.

THIS IS OUR WILL!

"*Repent." (i.e., turn away from SIN*)

*SIN: Disobedience to God (God's love way)

Ho.

Do I "cry in the wilderness?"

Red Elk

50732948R00034

Made in the USA
Lexington, KY
27 March 2016